LET IT BE FOR GOOD

A STORY OF REPEATED BROKENNESS AND RENEWAL WITH ORDINARY PEOPLE BEING USED IN EXTRAORDINARY CIRCUMSTANCES

Martha Gilreath

Copyright © 2020 Martha Gilreath.

All rights reserved. No part of this book may be used or reproduced by any means, graphic, electronic, or mechanical, including photocopying, recording, taping or by any information storage retrieval system without the written permission of the author except in the case of brief quotations embodied in critical articles and reviews.

This book is a work of non-fiction. Unless otherwise noted, the author and the publisher make no explicit guarantees as to the accuracy of the information contained in this book and in some cases, names of people and places have been altered to protect their privacy.

Archway Publishing books may be ordered through booksellers or by contacting:

Archway Publishing
1663 Liberty Drive
Bloomington, IN 47403
www.archwaypublishing.com
1 (888) 242-5904

Because of the dynamic nature of the Internet, any web addresses or links contained in this book may have changed since publication and may no longer be valid. The views expressed in this work are solely those of the author and do not necessarily reflect the views of the publisher, and the publisher hereby disclaims any responsibility for them.

Any people depicted in stock imagery provided by Getty Images are models, and such images are being used for illustrative purposes only. Certain stock imagery © Getty Images.

Unless otherwise noted, all Scripture quotations are from the ESV® Bible (The Holy Bible, English Standard Version®), copyright © 2001 by Crossway, a publishing ministry of Good News Publishers. Used by permission. All rights reserved.

Scripture quotations marked (NIV) are taken from the Holy Bible, New International Version®, NIV®. Copyright © 1973, 1978, 1984, 2011 by Biblica, Inc.™ Used by permission of Zondervan. All rights reserved worldwide. www.zondervan.comThe "NIV" and "New International Version" are trademarks registered in the United States Patent and Trademark Office by Biblica, Inc.™

ISBN: 978-1-4808-8894-4 (sc)
ISBN: 978-1-4808-8895-1 (e)

Library of Congress Control Number: 2020903933

Print information available on the last page.

Archway Publishing rev. date: 04/24/2020

To my family,
who have been willing to put themselves
on the line for the least of these.

Contents

Preface ix

Chapter 1   I Want to Be a Hero 1
Chapter 2   I Am Sorry with My Whole Heart 5
Chapter 3   Regret 16
Chapter 4   Broken Pieces Still Work
            Broken Crayons Still Color 28
Chapter 5   It Takes a Village 33
Chapter 6   What Just Happened? 38
Chapter 7   Sisters of the Heart 43
Chapter 8   DJJ or Us 56
Chapter 9   Stranded 61
Chapter 10 Purple Weave and Scabies! 65

Epilogue 71

Preface

As our nation struggles with escalating drug use our children are becoming staggering statistics in the foster care arena. Parents are being sucked under by addiction while our children end up living in unsafe homes where loved ones are not meeting their basic needs. More than four hundred thousand children are in foster care in the United States, according to the Department of Health and Human Services. The Adoption and Foster Care Analysis and Reporting System states that a foster child enters the system every two minutes. Wow! Those are astounding statistics when you think that each number represents an innocent child. Most children are removed due to neglect and abuse, with drug use being a common culprit. When a child goes into protective custody, it is a real struggle to find placement for him or her. A huge need for foster parents exists. Foster parents are adults that have proven to be capable of providing a safe home for children that are temporarily removed from their own homes. Case works and intake workers call one possibility after the other only to hear that foster homes are full or any number of other excuses for hours on end. Many times, the children end up in an overcrowded children's home or waiting in an office for hours on end. Many of our state workers fighting for the children are overwhelmed and underappreciated as they contest an ongoing battle where few victories are celebrated. The burnout rate is high in these professions, which makes the battle for the children even worse than ever as there is no consistency in the people on their team working together to decide and lay out the best plan for each child. Courts are backed up due to the volume of cases. Adoptions and/or reunifications take way longer than they should. It is a frustrating system that can become so focused on the paperwork that children become numbers, and cases are prolonged at the mercy of the court system. The children become victims again and again as everyone struggles to stretch a frail system and make it cover more than it can possibly take care of effectively.

What can we do to help? What can you do to help? In the Christian faith we know that Jesus stated that the greatest commandment is found in the Gospels. Mark 12:30–31 states, "Love the Lord your God with all your heart and with all your soul and with all your mind and with all your strength. The second is this: 'Love your neighbor as yourself.' There is no commandment greater than these." In the book of James, we are told to take care of widows and orphans. There are plenty of orphans and neighbors that as Christians we are called to help. There are a reported 240 million Christians in the United States. *Christianity Today* states that there are somewhere around 384,000 congregations in the United States. If each church undertook one child in foster care, we could provide for the least of these in unimaginable healthy ways. A certain few can't keep doing it alone. We need second shift. We need backup! I kept imagining a game of tag as I fostered for seven years. I am tired of running and would like to "tag" the next person to be "It."

The goal of this book is to give you a glimpse of real children in foster care and us as real people called to love and care for them. All the names in this story are fictitious, but the stories are real. The people in this book are not perfect, nor are any of the situations. I surely don't want to deceive anyone about the realities of caring for hurting children. It is not easy. However, it is good. If we all take a turn, it can be done with excellence and honor to our heavenly Father. It takes the removal of self and an acknowledgment to the Source of our love and strength. It entails a strong yes to God if He is calling you to take on this amazing opportunity.

For Good

>Kristin Chenoweth, Idina Menzel, Stephen Schwartz, Lee Lessack

I've heard it said
That people come into our lives for a reason
Bringing something we must learn
And we are led

To those who help us most to grow

Who can say if I've been changed for the better?
But because I knew you
I have been changed for good

CHAPTER 1
I Want to Be a Hero

*Therefore, He is able to save completely
those who come to God through him,
because he always lives to intercede for them.
—Hebrews 7:25*

Who doesn't want to be a hero? When I think of the word *hero*, the first things that pop into my mind are Superman stopping a moving train, Batman and Robin taking down the Joker before he destroys Gotham City, and don't forget Wonder Woman fighting fearlessly in a war to end all wars. Or I have visions of the movie *Footloose* with Kevin Bacon playing chicken on the tractor and the song "I Need a Hero" playing, cheering him on. I am not sure what the point of playing Chicken on tractors was or what good could come from that, but nevertheless the song blares in my head when I say the word *hero* out loud. Who doesn't want to be a hero, right? Heroes are loved and admired. They are brave, respected, and fearless! They save people!

So many people think foster parents are heroes, and in a big sense, they are. We were a foster family, and *hero* would be a stretch as an adjective to describe us. I am about as average as a person could ever be. Not fat but not skinny, not pretty but not ugly, not rich but not poor, not smart but not dumb, not mean but not always nice either. Just plain old average. But God took this average and used it in extraordinary ways.

Children in foster care need a hero to rescue them. When we first began fostering, perhaps I thought it would be an opportunity to be a hero for some of the least of these. However, as we journeyed through the foster system, we experienced so many failures and sad stories and fewer victories and feelings of being a hero. It could become too much to handle until you make yourself stop and realize who the real hero in the story is, and what that means to each of us. Jesus is our Hero, and He is equipping us to be the tools for Him because He loves these children more than we could ever love them. You don't have to be anything special to be a foster parent. If you are being called to foster, He will equip you.

Foster care is not for everyone. I, however, could see how God had softened my heart toward this opportunity and how He had equipped us for the challenge.

He made sure I had a model of what it looks like to step in and help a family out because my parents modeled this to our family. He gave me a background in the schools, so I knew the ins and outs of helping these children succeed in the classroom. He gave me a platform in the church to immerse these children in knowledge of Him. He gave me a man that, maybe reluctantly, came beside me and allowed our family to pursue fostering. He put me with an alcoholic and a drug addict who I loved so that I would have empathy for all the moms I would soon work with. He made me confident in chaos because that is what I was about to be involved in full time. God is so good! Don't you see it?

Even though I knew God was calling us to foster, I experienced fear and doubt. I had all the normal questions and doubts. "Will my children get hurt? What if the other children do or say inappropriate things? What if we get too attached?" My favorite fear was, "What if we get a pyromaniac, and they burn our house down?" Trust me, the fears, doubts, and questions went on and on. Satan was unashamedly trying to get my attention off what God had called us to do. It was maddening. My head and my heart were in constant conflict. My family, however, lean toward being adventure junkies, and we were warming up to the idea of the biggest adventure we had encountered thus far. We began to get excited about this endeavor and in we dove headfirst into the dirty, murky, unknown waters of fostering. These waters took us down lots of times, and I thought we wouldn't get back up. Other times they refreshed us and gave new life. These waters became our life and the lives of about forty-two foster children that took the ride with us. May these glimpses into the lives of the foster children that came through our home inspire you to take chances, dream big, and lean on the one that equips and saves us each and every time. He is our Hero!

> *People were also bringing babies to Jesus to have him touch them. When the disciples saw this, they rebuked them. But Jesus called the children to him and said, "Let the little children come to me, and do not hinder them, for the kingdom of God belongs to such as these." (Luke 18:15–16)*

As we look at Luke 18 above, it says that the people were trying to get the children to Jesus so He could touch them. Two things stand out to me in this reading. First, Jesus had not been crucified or resurrected. Yet they seemed to understand His power. His touch was what they needed for the children. They fought their way through the crowd to get them to Him.

Next, I notice that scripture didn't say "their parents" it says "people." We are the people! If not me or you, then who? Satan is trying to get the children too. There are some whacked foster parents out there. Go to a foster parent meeting, and you will be alarmed at the different types of people meeting this call. Listen to some stories from some of the foster children. We need strong

Christian foster parents to get the children to Jesus. It will not just automatically happen.

I worked in the school system and felt that my hands were tied so many times as I worked to give children and parents tools for healthier lifestyles. I loved the children and felt equipped to handle them but feeling burnt out by putting on the 'band-aids' and sending them on their way. I began to see fostering as a perfect opportunity to show the children Jesus. To show them love through our family and pray it would flow over into their souls, and they would recognize the source of the Love as the Father. As Christians, are we fighting to get the children to Jesus? In the age of helicopter parenting I see more and more adults so focused on their own children that they lose sight of the other children that are all around them. It breaks my heart, and I can't imagine what it does to the Father's heart. They are all precious in His sight, we must remember—not just our children, but *the* children.

We have gotten dirty, hurt, scarred, and stretched along the way. We have never felt abandoned by the Father nor that we weren't doing what we were supposed to be doing. All our children saw glimpses of God. He has planted seeds, and we trust Him to grow them in His time. On this earth we may not even see the effects of their time with us. I am praying *big*, though! I am praying that unhealthy cycles will be broken, and generations will come to know our true Hero through these children who have been in our home.

CHAPTER 2

I Am Sorry with My Whole Heart

Produce fruit in keeping with repentance.
—*Luke 3:8*

I wish you could hear these words audibly, the way I hear them in my head, the way this precious four-year-old said them to me. "I am sorry with my whole heart, Miss M."

On August 30, 2012, our family became a certified foster family. We had taken our time with the process. Our children were older (one in college), and we were ready to "jump in." It honestly felt a little more like a free fall than an intentional jump, but nonetheless, we were in!

We decided as a family to do one or two children at a time, and they would need to be school age children and younger than our youngest at the time. That gave us a range of about six years to twelve years, which seemed reasonable for us.

By lunchtime that day, we had a call about two siblings, ages one and three. I hadn't known what to expect when you get "the call." "We have two siblings that have been removed from their home for …," the caller said. "Would you be willing to take them?" How could I say no to that? Everything in me began planning on changing our lives around to accommodate two babies. Of course, I was willing! Thankfully though, something made me stop and think, *Call your husband.* I did, and everything in him said *no*! He reminded me that those were not the ages we agreed to take. I called DSS back and repeated what my husband had said. I was miserable wondering what would happen to those babies. Who would take them? How must they feel? I was even mad at my husband for sticking to the plan.

Well, I didn't get to fret for long because as we were walking out the door to take our youngest to soccer practice, we got another call. This time the DSS placement worker said, "We have two brothers, ages four and five that were removed from school and not allowed to return because a meth lab was found in the backyard. They have been sitting in the DSS office all day. Maybe you could get them for just the night?" Again, I talked to my husband and again he said, "That isn't what we agreed on."

I don't know how, but I convinced him to just give them a try for the night or until DSS was able to find a placement. Thus began our calling to foster. It was messy, dirty, confusing, inspiring, heartbreaking, spontaneous, thrilling, aggravating, offensive, upsetting, and so much more!

The placement person connected us to a transporter, and we were instructed where to meet. It is hard to describe our conversations for the next hour or so. We left the house giving our girls instructions on what to do to get things ready, took one to soccer, and drove to the meeting place. On the way, my husband and I were a bundle of nerves. What should we say? Do we hug them? What should they call us? Are they going to be crying and fighting not to go? So many questions! Also, the adrenaline rush to deal with. Holy cow! We are getting two little boys whom we have never met, and we are meeting in a parking lot to move them from one stranger to two other strangers. It felt like a drug deal or an illegal something. I don't know. Everything was just so surreal.

Could this really be how it is done? *Is this real life?* This was our first glimpse at how dirty and broken this journey would be. A dark, deserted parking lot, getting two little boys carrying only their book bags, scared to death to go with these complete strangers did not lend toward a story of happily ever after. We signed a paper, took the book bags, and buckled our two new little ones into the back of the car. That was it. We were on our own and terrified!

These little ones had gone to school that day expecting nothing. They had no idea that life as they knew it was about to be turned upside down. They were picked up from school by a Department of Social Services (DSS) caseworker, put in a car and taken to the DSS headquarters. A different worker called possible placement homes all afternoon until trying us. We were a last resort. They knew we wanted older children, but they were desperate. It was getting late, and the children needed to sleep after such an exhausting day. We were to keep them for just a few days until they found someone else. By now, we have heard this statement quite a few times, and it is a relative term. It can really mean a few days, a few weeks, or a few months!

Well, these little boys claimed a place in our hearts right from the start. The experience was raw. Fostering children ripped us open emotionally in ways I had never thought possible. It was an exposing of ourselves and our hearts that we could never have imagined, and I cannot adequately describe it now. The little ones that came through our home had been hurt in unimaginable ways. They were scared and alone. All my protective, mama bear senses heightened. It is like I put up an invisible fence around these children, and I stood guard, daring anyone to try to hurt them on my watch. I was rough on the schools and my family when I felt like there were any derogatory or unfair comments or situations put in their paths. I wanted this time with us to be a time of refreshing and healing. I said the best thing I could think of to say that first night to those children and to each child since; they are words we all need to hear from time to time. "You are safe." Can't you just hear Jesus telling you that right now? "You are safe, child!" We watched them visibly relax. We can visibly relax too as this truth resonates in our souls. God tells us over and over in His word that He has got this!

These boys had never been away from home. They were four and five years old, scared, and in an unfamiliar setting. They needed us to be safe. That is true of so many of us, isn't it? We are going along just fine until—*wham!* Something happens that shakes our world. We grasp for something to help us, something that will ease our pain, make us hurt less, and give us hope. We make bad choices as to what can help us, and our circumstances get worse. Our only hope is Jesus! Sometimes we don't need Him until He is *all* we need. Ben Rector has a song called "When a Heart Breaks," and the lyrics say:

> *This isn't easy,*
> *This isn't clear,*
> *And you don't need Jesus until you're here.*

So many times, it is our hopelessness that turns us to our *hope*—Jesus!

Our hope was in that car on the way home that night. He guided our conversations, and we all began to just relax. We introduced ourselves and told the boys about our family and what they could expect at our house. Since the boys only had their book bags with them, we needed to make a stop for some clothes and necessities. We are from a small town, and our best option was the Dollar General that night. We ran in and grabbed pajamas, underwear, pull-ups (just in case), socks, an outfit for the next day, toothbrushes, etc. We finished all of this just in time to pick up from soccer and then head home. The boys were feeling more and more comfortable. There was a lot of chatter in the car.

Once we got home it was getting late, but the girls were so excited and wanted to show the boys around. Then, my parents came over to meet our new "family members." They were as excited and committed as we were. These were the first "fostergrands," and the boys took to 'Geej' and 'PR' at once. Since that night they have been PR and Geej to at least forty more children. They have modeled love and support to us and each child who has entered our home. We could not have taken this journey without them! Everyone needs a village, and they were our core!

We finally got the boys bathed and into bed. By the time I lay down, I was exhausted. I was expecting to be up and down with the boys all night since they were in unfamiliar territory. They did not move! That night nor any other night in the last seven years has a child woke me up in the middle of the night. God knew I have my own night issues, and I couldn't handle more, perhaps. Whatever the reason, I am grateful.

Our home is busy. With four children who all love sports and time with friends, a husband who works too much, and my involvement in many things, we don't really stop. It turned out that the boys' first weekend with us was going to be one of our busiest weekends of all. Every Labor Day for as long as I can remember my family hosts a huge dove shoot and barbecue. It is always insanely busy as we prepare for hundreds of people and usually a full house of extras with cousins coming in from all over. Well, the boys were doing great taking all of this in, and I was trying to be careful with them and this stimuli overload. There were hundreds of people, music, guns, hunting, food, and tons of kids.

On Sunday, about forty of our closest family members came over to eat lunch and swim. Some of the teens decided to ride four-wheelers around the farm. The rest of us were outside preparing to swim when suddenly I heard this horrible crash! I flew through the field in my bathing suit and bare feet (not an attractive sight) until I found the ATV flipped over on its side. Teenagers were crying and panicked. We called 911 and two ambulances arrived. Amid the chaos and confusion, I ran upstairs to change so that I could get to the hospital. On my way up I happened to glance back down at our pool area, and what I saw stopped me in my tracks. I saw my entire beautiful family holding hands and praying. I dropped to my knees then and there and thanked my God! I was offered a glimpse of peace, and God's hand reached out to me and mine through the prayers of those beautiful people crying out on our behalf.

While our cousin had a difficult injury and recovery, she is fine now. The others just had some scrapes and bruises and a *big* scare. Once we were all home and recovered, I thought back on that weekend and smiled. These little boys had a story to tell about their first week in foster care. They could easily say they were placed in a home where there was a big party, lots of loud people, guns, ambulances, wrecks, four-wheelers, and no telling what else. But my prayer was that what they would remember was a group of people crying out to the Lord in their time of need, knowing He was in control and taking care of their loved ones. May they remember a family joining hands and praying around a pool during crisis. Please, Father, let this be what they remember. May that prayer impact them more than the chaos. I haven't had a report filed against me yet, so I am thinking all is well.

For the next eight weeks these little boys immersed themselves into our family. They went to many more soccer games and tennis matches than they ever wanted to see. They went to church, did farm activities, went to pumpkin patches and the zoo, and had so many more life experiences. Asa, our five-year-old, went to 5K kindergarten while Bobby went to our church preschool until a spot opened for him in our district. A friend of mine also volunteered to help with Bobby since 4K school was just half a day. I was still doing my part-time job and had already committed to doing a maternity leave for the guidance counselor who had taken my place at my old job. Life was busy, and I was thankful for a strong support system.

The first thirty days of a new placement is fondly referred to as "the honeymoon period." After that, reality begins to set in, and behaviors and attitudes can start to become more challenging. These little boys wanted their mommy, and my biological children struggled with their own space issues. I have never been good with whiny children and did not allow my own children to get by with much whining. It seemed that God wanted to grow me in this area and was using this pet peeve to teach me now. I had never heard whining to this degree, and it was wearing on me. Things in my neat little world were turned upside down.

One night everyone had a meeting or a sporting event, and I knew it was going to be a late night. I asked one of my daughter's friends to babysit for a couple of hours. When I got home, she was more than a little frazzled. It turned out that Asa had deliberately tinkled all over his room. I mean just stood there and pulled his pants down and peed everywhere. Then, he drew all over the bed and the wall. They had both scorned bedtime and had dropped off to sleep right before I got home. Our sweet friend would most probably never have a soft spot in her heart for fostering. Never had the boys been this defiant, and it reminded me their need for consistency as they battled for a sense of control in a life that felt out of control. We all leaned in harder and stronger, and the boys leveled back out and seemed to thrive. Even the whining got a teeny bit better.

Both boys were sweet and loving by nature. They loved to cuddle and be loved. They wanted to please others and did not like for you to be unhappy with them. One day I got the most precious apology I have ever gotten, and I think of it quite often. "I am sorry with my whole heart, Miss M." Bobby had done something—I don't remember his offense—that had gotten him into trouble, but I remember these words over and over. Not just sorry, but "sorry with my whole heart." I say them to my Savior when I know I have been wrong, and then I don't think He remembers my offense either, just the attitude of my repentance. Haven't we all done this? Done something wrong and then with our entire being we wish that we could take it back?

Regret—the word that shapes so many of our lives and drives us places we didn't mean to go. The dictionary defines regret as feeling sad, repentant, or disappointed over (something that has happened or been done, especially a loss or missed opportunity).

Repentance: the act of reviewing one's actions and feeling contrition or regret for past wrongs, which is accompanied by commitment to change for the better.

If regret is shaping your life right now, don't let it have that power. Move toward repentance and leave regret behind. Jesus is holding out His hand for you. Just reach out and take hold! Don't you know so many of the men and women in the Bible felt and experienced these words? Think of David, Rahab, Zacchaeus, Moses, Paul, and the list goes on and on. Regret could have ended things for them, but God Himself used them in mighty ways. He delivered them from the pit of regret and hopelessness, and He will do that for us. He wants to use us all in mighty ways!

J. D. Greear's book *Gospel* includes a gospel prayer. Part 1 says, "In Christ there's nothing I can do that would make Him love me more, and there's nothing I've done that could make Him love me less." He loves you completely just as you are! He can't love you less! He loves you already!

Now, I mentioned drugs as the culprit for the boy's removal. It

turns out that the mom didn't really know what dad was doing in the backyard. Nor would she have thought it would have put her at the risk of losing the boys. This may seem as foreign to you as it docs to me, but to many, this is real life. It is generational. The poverty, the drugs, and the hopelessness are all that is known to so many families. Fostering these children is such a chance to break that cycle, if there is any chance at all.

The decisions that cost this mama her boys could have thrown her into the "pit of regret." She could have stayed there in the pit among the company of blaming others, despair, playing the victim, drugs, alcohol, or several other things to help dull her pain and help her not to feel the responsibility of the blame. Well, let me tell you, these boys' mom did an about face. She has been the best mom I have seen in the foster care arena. The gospels tell the story of a lady wanting healing from Jesus. Her faith in who He was allowed her to just reach out and touch the hem of his cloak to experience healing. She touched His hem amid the chaos and confusion, and it changed her. (Mark 5:28, Luke 8:43–45, Matthew 9:20.) She experienced His power and His love for her and her boys when she reached for Him. She experienced forgiveness. She stood up strong! She jumped into the fight to get her boys back under the wings of Jesus (Psalm 91) and fought like a mama bear. She called DSS every day. She didn't let their case get put on the back burner. She figured out what she had to do, and she did it. All classes and sessions were completed as thoroughly and quickly as possible. She accepted responsibility and blamed only herself. She rose up stronger than ever. She went to the church for support and found it. She spoke to younger ladies and gave her testimony openly in hopes of helping others not get in a similar situation. To this day, forty children later, she is the only birth mother who has ever written my family a thank-you note or said thank you at all. I still have the note. It is precious to me. She is also only one of two parents with whom the courts have allowed the children to go back into the home. Everyone else we have had has gone to different family members or placement.

Eight weeks after they had arrived, the boys were going to get to go home. I was expecting them to be a little sadder about leaving us than they were, and my feelings, I must admit, were hurt a little. Now that I have been here awhile, I understand better that there is nothing like the love a child has for his parent, even parents who don't deserve this love or reciprocate it. It is love born out of familiarity, dependency, survival, and loyalty, for the most part it seems.

We went into the foster care arena with the goal of reunification. That means our goal was to be a safe, healthy place for children to live while family members got their stuff together in order to get the kids back. We were not in to adopt. We have four children of our own, and that is enough for us. However, I was not expecting the depth of love I would feel for the children who came through our home. We were their advocates; we fought for their good; we clothed them, fed them, disciplined them, hugged them, wiped their tears, tucked them in at night, read to them, and loved them with a love that we pray points them to Jesus. They were dependent on us, and bonds formed quickly. I was not expecting the news that they would be leaving to hit me so hard. In their case I got the news they were leaving one day, and they were gone the next. They were happy, their mama was thrilled, and we were happy too, but *ouch!* It hurt! A piece of my heart was broken, and it just hurt.

Once they moved home, their mom let them call us a few times. I had become her cheerleader, so it was good to hear from her and especially to know that the boys were fine. About a month later we asked if we could deliver some Christmas gifts to them. She said that would be fine, so all six of us drove about an hour toward the mountains until we got to their house. The house screamed of poverty. When we drove up the drive, it was to a home that I would normally be wary of entering. The boys came out to meet us. They were a little shy at first but quickly warmed up. They invited us in. The porch was treacherous to walk across with missing and rotten boards. Inside there were some bare spots in the carpet and only the bare necessities. What I noticed the most, however, was that this house was clean, and this mama was proud of her home and especially her boys. She wanted me to know that they were safe and loved, and I appreciated her caring enough about me and my family to let us in for that reason. She was doing the best she could do. My heart soared for this family. They were going to make it, and I just couldn't get over the fact that God had allowed us to be a part of their story! Their story, our story ... His story.

It was so good!

CHAPTER 3

REGRET

God intended it all for good.
—Genesis 50:20

This story is painful and evokes feelings of guilt and uncertainty till this day. It reminds me of Genesis 50:20. Joseph was put in an unfair situation where he was sold into slavery and then placed in jail for a crime he did not commit. God took Joseph from the pain and the prison and raised him up to the palace. The story didn't even stop with Joseph's blessings but goes on to allow Joseph to bless his brothers with food, family, financial security, and mostly forgiveness for the wrongs they had done. God can do this kind of stuff.

Though we didn't mean to hurt this child, he was hurt. It is important to remind ourselves that God is bigger than the hurt and can turn it for good! He can use our insufficiencies for good. He knows our mistakes from the beginning, and He is prepared. He is not surprised. I am praying that He brings this child up from the ashes and that his story is beautiful!

> *To bestow on them a crown of beauty instead of ashes, the oil of gladness instead of mourning, and a garment of praise instead of a spirit of despair. (Isaiah 61:3)*

Anyway, here it goes. For the next month or so we provided respite care, but mostly it was just us in recovery mode. Respite care is when you provide short-term care for a child. The foster parents may need a babysitter for the weekend, or a home where a child is being moved may need a few days before they can take him or her. We provided that support a few times over the next month. During one of these respite times we were introduced to a "game-changer." He changed us all from the inside out, I would say. I will call him Devonta.

When DSS called to see if we could keep a child from our area while his foster mom went on a retreat for the weekend, we were like sure, a weekend. Well, when I told my friend who we were getting, she became very concerned. He was one of her students, and he was not an easy one. His experiences of neglect, physical abuse, and drug abuse by his family had made him emotionally unstable, and sometimes she was even afraid of this fifth-grader. Well, we could survive a weekend, and we would just watch him closely.

He came into our house with confidence, like he had been here before and knew us all. He was funny and full of personality. He and my youngest bonded from the start. We went hiking in the mountains, and he got separated from us for a minute. The tale he painted of that minute of despair had us all in stitches. Hmmm … where was his crazy? It wasn't standing out; I think it was just blending with ours.

A few weeks later the foster mom asked us to keep him again for a short time. He stayed for another weekend, and not long after he had gone home, she called back. "Devonta is more than I can handle as a single, working mom. He needs a father figure and more children to play with. Would your family be interested in keeping him?" Well, we talked about it and decided we could do it. We worked with DSS to make the change official.

Devonta moved in at Thanksgiving of that year. He began

calling us Momma and Daddy right off the bat. There was no plan to place him back with his family. His parents were out of the picture. He did have two sisters that he saw once a month for a two-hour visit. He craved family. He moved in, and we never skipped a beat. He felt at home, and he added so many flavors to our family. We all fell in love with this beautiful boy.

Christmas came, and he had his first meltdown. Can you imagine being twelve years old and away from all that you knew and the people that you loved for Christmas? He disappeared after we opened the gifts, and I found him in his room crying. He had loved his gifts. He and my son had each gotten a new bike, nerf guns, and clothes. His favorite gift of all was the BB gun my youngest had bought him with his own money. He wanted Devonta to have something that every little boy in the country had and in my son's eyes, needed. Devonta was thrilled. So then why was he in his room crying? He was overwhelmed; all that he had experienced, all that he had lost, and all that he had gained just swept over him for a time and overwhelmed him. He didn't know what to do with this flood of emotion, so he just wept. I held him, and we both wept. I prayed over him and longed to take away his pain, but all I could do was rock him back and forth and pray he felt the love of his Father in heaven loving him through me.

The week after Christmas we went to the beach with my in-laws. Devonta had never been to the beach before, so to get to see it for the first time through his eyes was something we all cherished. He was beyond excited! He didn't know how to swim, so I was nervous. However, this house was unlike any we had ever stayed at nor have we since. It was magnificent! The living area was huge with glass covering the entire back wall that overlooked the ocean. Doors opened onto a deck with a hot tub and pool area that included the coolest waterfall ever. We all were in awe, but Devonta was in heaven! He learned to swim that week, and he earned the nickname, Hot Tub. He stayed in the hot tub swimming the entire time, getting out only when we made it mandatory.

Once January came and school started back, the honeymoon period was over, and real life hit! He was being immersed in new experiences such as Upward Basketball, soccer, studying, family mealtime, working on a farm, church, mission trips, and what it looks like to function in a somewhat normal family. He was thriving, and everyone around him was falling in love with this kid! He made an impact on so many people from all walks of life.

He saved the meltdowns for home and mostly for me. We had some major struggles and setbacks. Devonta and I were equally stubborn and could bring out the worst in each other. On several occasions I had to remind him that no matter what, I was the adult, and my way would trump his way. I am not sure that was the best way to approach the issues he had, but I think it gave him some peace. No matter how mad he would get, nor what kind of fit he would pitch, he could rest in the fact that it was not going to be more than I could handle. His lack of control would not dictate the outcome of the situation. With society screaming at us to let everyone just be who they want to be, it seems that parents think that means they shouldn't parent. Our children are begging for limits and boundaries. They will push and push until finally, when it is too late, a parent will try to step in with a punishment of some sort. By this time unmeasurable amount of damage has been done and a child will spend much of their adult life trying to recover from terrible choices that were made because no one was helping them make wise decisions while their frontal lobe was trying to form. I never let on to him, but sometimes I felt like it was more than I could handle. On those days I could literally lean into the arms of my Savior, and He could always handle it. It was as if I could hear His gentle whisper: "I've got this!"

I am about to get on a soapbox here. One thing I have noticed through the years is the growing need society has to label our young people. They have anxiety, anger issues, fears, learning problems, behavior defiant disorder, attention deficient, hyperactivity, and the list goes on and on. Why do we do this? Is it to make us as parents feel like we are not failing in parenting when we can turn their behaviors into medical problems? I am a special education major, and I know there are real medical issues that children are born with, but I am now seeing more than medical issues. So many parents are slapping a label on their kids and saying, "Oh, well!" Then they try to make their world and everyone else's world revolve around little Johnny's issues. This is setting those kids up for failure as adults. In the real world, everyone is *not* going to try to please little Johnny. They won't care what his label says he is when he is working a job to support his family. Little Johnny needs to know he can cope and succeed, and this starts at home at an early age. It takes a ton of work and effort by the people with whom God has surrounded these children. It is much easier to sit back and just give in to the child, but, then, we are not parenting. We have to equip our children and give them tools to help success be obtainable for them. Otherwise, they will reach a point where mom and dad can't protect them and they will only fail.

Devonta and plenty of our other foster children have come to us and tried to use their label to get out of a situation. The most popular cop-out for us has been, "I have anger issues!" They say it like that should explain everything, or better yet, it should scare *us* into submission. I will never forget the first time Devonta screamed it at us. He screamed it with authority and finality, as if he was playing a game of chess, and he had just "checked" us. The situation should be over! Well, my ever-calm, Alpha of the house husband got right in his face and said, "I have anger issues too! Deal with it!" I don't remember Devonta using that threat again. He still had anger, as he had a right to from what all he had been through, but it wasn't going to define him. We worked on coping skills, and he learned to time himself out when he needed to. He learned to adjust and succeed.

He had a ton of other issues, too. He had learning disabilities, which were real, and he had real emotional problems and attention deficit disorder. He had a lot to work through! I did not expect him to do this alone or by me just hoping it would automatically happen. We all got in the trenches and worked our behinds off. I sat in classes with him; I spoke to teachers; I went to meetings, and I sat at the table with him for hours in the afternoons doing homework. I stood strong when I wanted to quit and give up. It was emotionally and physically draining. It would have been easier to say, "Oh, well, this isn't my kid. He is already this way, and there is nothing I can do about it. It's too late for him." It would have been easier not to care about this kid or his future, but God gave me a desire for Devonta to succeed as an adult. I knew I wouldn't have him forever, so I poured in!

I can't remember where I heard this or who said it, but I think of it often.

> *It is not our job to raise happy children,*
> *but it is our job to raise healthy adults.*

This child of God deserves a healthy life not tainted by how the world labeled him but by how God designed him. I wanted him to see himself as the strong, funny, lovable, resilient young man he could become.

He was hard! He made me madder than I thought I could get sometimes. I may have developed my own anger issues during this time. Our own children received plenty of spankings when they were younger. As foster parents, we are not allowed to spank. We had to get very creative with realistic and suitable punishment that fit each offense. I wish I had written them down because it was some pretty creative stuff that I could have shared. One of the ones I remember was picking up rocks. We live on a farm, and it seems we grow rocks. We would be millionaires if we could think of a way to make money off of all the rocks we have in our fields that need to be smooth and rock free. Taking a bucket out into the field and filling it with rocks and then hauling it to a ditch somewhere became a great way to release stress, reflect, and get it together. I also remember a pair of socks that he *loved*, and he would lose the right to wear them for certain reasons. It seems crazy, but it motivated him to correct some behaviors, so we went with it. My friend still can't get over it today. Socks? Really? Children need an adult who loves them and will fight with them to help them realize they can be in control of their actions and attitudes and that we will love them through the process. They need to know they are capable and equipped to make good choices and benefit themselves and others in this life. Don't give up, friend, if you are in the trenches with your little one now. Dig deep, lean it, and *don't* give up! It isn't easy. It's life.

Parental rights were terminated, and Devonta was adoptable. We wanted him. My children loved him. We all loved him. We wanted him as a part of our forever family. My husband was very firm though in the fact that he did not feel led to adopt. I have never understood his stance on this, but as the leader in our home, I respected this decision. I prayed that no one would want to adopt him and that he could just stay with us. We explained to Devonta that we were not in the position to adopt but that he could stay with us forever unless God sent the perfect family that would legally adopt him. I secretly thought that no one would want to adopt a now sixth-grader with so many issues. I felt safe in the fact that he would stay with us.

God had other plans, though. A newlywed couple was interested. They came to visit. They took him to their house for weekends. I told them all of the struggles, and they knew his history. They decided they wanted to adopt him. I begged DSS and the adoption lady to just leave him. I told them this couple had not been married long enough to handle him. I told them that we were all happy and good and that he could stay with us forever, but they were dead set on adoption. It is like they became angry that we wouldn't adopt, and they were dead set on having him moved. The code word was a "forever family," and that was only obtained through adoption in their eyes. When I told him the news, he said, "I knew this would happen." It was awful. We all cried yet tried to be encouraging at the same time. It was a month-long transition. We went to the beach for a last family time together. We had a *big* party at our church for all his family and friends to celebrate his adoption. The new family, along with at least one hundred other people from our community, came to share their warm wishes for the best future ever. It was as good as it could be, and Devonta seemed happy and good with all of it. I guess he was used to things going differently than expected, and it was just another hand that life dealt him, and he would just roll with it. It was the only time I saw him being submitted in a difficult situation.

On the last day, the new family wanted to pick him up from school instead of from our home. Their family therapist recommended this transition as a better solution. Our children said their goodbyes for the hundredth time as they headed out the door that morning. I was very worried about how this would affect them, especially my youngest. He and Devonta were so close and truly loved each other. They had plans to room together at college, and they talked of this as Devonta and he hugged goodbye. It was heart-wrenching and forever ingrained in our minds.

I drove him to school later on the ATV to try to lighten the mood. (We live in a small town and riding an ATV to school is not unheard of). I reminded him of God's plans for him and how loved he was as a child of the King. He had been introduced to Jesus while in our home and been baptized at our church. I prayed over him and held him. He did not cry. He was calm and took it all as if it was just another part of his life, and he expected nothing more. We had all been assured that we would still be able to get together frequently. It wasn't supposed to really be goodbye, just see you later. However, I knew it would be different, and maybe something in me knew it would be goodbye. It is hard to say how I grieved. My heart was broken. I felt like we had failed him, I felt judged because we were not adopting; I was angry, and I felt loss that was real and painful. I went to the mountains for a while to get away and fall into the arms of my Savior.

> *He heals the brokenhearted and binds up their wounds.*
> *(Psalm 147:3)*

It was a safe place away from judgment and hurt. I prayed we were not outside of His will for our family or for this child.

What he had been told would happen with the new family and what actually happened were two different things. When a child loses trust, it changes things. It turned out we were allowed to meet him at a park only one other time. We had a great time and thought all was well. However, he still called us Mama and Daddy, and it bothered the new parents. They talked to their therapist, and it was decided that we should not be allowed contact anymore. Another situation out of Devonta's control was decided, and he was the loser again. He was fighting back the only way he knew how, and it was costing him. Things at his new home were not going well.

While he was with us, he had monthly visits with his two older sisters. During the summer they came to our house to swim and eat and just play together. The caseworkers, the guardian ad litems, the children, and my crew would eat together and talk. It was important for them to see each other. They loved each other, and they were all they had left of their birth family. This important component was also taken from Devonta when he moved. They decided his older sister's behaviors were not good for him, so visitations were cut out. All of his "lifelines" were now severed, and he was left to maneuver in new territory with no support from the known sources of his past life. It was traumatic. He was failed.

I didn't hear from the adopted mom for a few months, and then one morning right before school was ending for the summer I was sitting in the parking lot about to walk into a store when she called. I was surprised when I realized she was calling, and I answered quickly. Without much preliminary ado, she briefly filled me in on what had been happening. Devonta had been acting out in very disturbing ways. She was expecting, she and her husband had decided not to adopt, and now they had moved him to another foster home. I tried not to say much. I remember thinking to myself, "Don't judge; don't speak; just listen. God, help me just listen and breathe." When we hung up, I sat in my car and cried.

DSS is a broken system. There are so many problems and not enough workers. Many of the workers are new and inexperienced. The turnover rate is high in these jobs. I try to be patient with the workers and realize they are not God. They are, for the most part, young and without many life experiences. But this time I was so angry at the system, and I wanted answers. This child had been added to the statistics of young, black, fatherless, homeless males who end up in jail or on the streets. I felt that DSS had moved him from us more to win some sort of adoption power struggle than to benefit him. They knew us and our hearts for Devonta. They had been in our home for countless hours during home visits and family visits with his sisters. They knew he was loved and happy with us. They had witnessed all the hurdles we had overcome; they had seen him experience success and growth. Yet, they insisted on parading him to all the adoption fairs and getting something on paper that finalized their end to the involvement with him.

This was a major setback from which it would be hard for him to recover. I couldn't believe this was happening. As soon as I got home, I called his caseworker. She was very upset that I had gotten word of the change in plans. It was very evident that neither she nor her department had wanted us to know of this development. I also found out they had decided not to tell him he was moving until that day. They just showed up and took him to a new foster home two hours away. No warning—no nothing.

I couldn't understand why they would not have notified us and put him back in our home. With every move that a child makes in the foster care system, the chances of him succeeding diminish. Why add another home to his file? They said it was because his behaviors in the previous home had been so disturbing that it had moved him to the therapeutic level of care. He could no longer be in normal foster care. I think that was a cover-up too. We called the state department several times to no avail. My husband and I met with the heads of DSS in our county and Devonta's, but they would not change their stance. They wanted him adopted or nothing. Well, nothing is what he got. Five years later he is still in foster care. We are friends on Facebook, and his posts are very dark and disturbing. He is a lost child. Much different than what he could have been. It breaks my heart. In so many arenas, paperwork is the deciding factor in all outcomes. Common sense has been replaced by how something looks on paper. In this case, the goal of the state was adoption because that looks good on paper. Devonta was failed.

At some point during our countless hours at the table working, I wrote the words, *VICTIM* and *VICTOR* on flashcards. I showed Devonta how similar the words were and that he had the power to decide what he would be. He could live as a victim, or he could rise up as a victor! We did this activity many days during a pity party or a meltdown. Looking back, I see how badly he was victimized by the system, his family, and even us. I pray that God will raise him up, that his ending will change much like the endings of those two words, that he will remember who he is as a son of the King, and that he will change generations. God promises He can do that, and I am choosing to trust that all of this bad will work out for Devonta's good.

> *No, in all these things we are more than conquerors through him who loved us. (Romans 8:37)*

Anyway, those who want to judge us, jump on in. I judge myself too. Why didn't we adopt him? I think our children judge us too. They guard themselves now as we get other children. They don't give their hearts away so freely anymore. It hurt too badly. We are all wounded. My husband does not feel like we were wrong. He still has not felt convicted that we should have adopted. He is probably right. He is a Christian and does seek God's voice and direction for our lives. He did not feel God leading us to adopt, and I will trust Him. I do feel like when my days on earth are done, I will kneel at the throne of my Father, and He will reveal what could have been to me—good or bad, right or wrong.

> *And we know that for those who love God all things work together for good, for those who are called according to his purpose. (Romans 8:28)*

Devonta knows God. He reminded us on Facebook once that we had introduced him to the love of our Father. I know God is in control of all things. He can move mountains, and the wind and water obey Him. He can work this out too. I was just a vessel, and I pray that it was enough.

> *Please, Lord, let the seeds planted in this child take root and grow him closer to you and your plans for him! Move him from victim to victor. Amen.*

CHAPTER 4

BROKEN PIECES STILL WORK
BROKEN CRAYONS STILL COLOR

*Let me hear joy and gladness; let the
bones that you have broken rejoice.*
—Psalm 51:8

Sometime between the second respite for Devonta and the time when his previous foster mom asked us to keep him full time, we took in two more brothers. They were the same ages as our first set of foster brothers, four and five years old. We will call them Finn and Garrett. The night they walked in our door; I remember being overcome with sorrow. The five-year-old was completely bent over with scoliosis. The DSS placement worker had left that fact out. He was also legally blind, required occupational therapy, physical therapy, and speech, and he had learning disabilities. I went to IEP (Individualized Educational Plan) meetings with more components than I had seen during the years that I worked in the school district. Pretty much every disability the school could handle was wrapped up in this one five-year-old. An IEP meeting usually included about three school personnel and a district person. Well, Finn's meetings consisted of five school personnel, three district people, and two outside agencies. It was a packed house, all working for and coming to the aid of this one little boy.

At a glance this little boy seemed broken, but he had no idea. He could do anything any other five-year-old could do. He was spunky and full of life and adventure. Both boys were a treat for our family! Again, hard work, time consuming, and they brought issues to the table, but they were just a joy for our family. One of the first days they were with us, we were out in the yard, and they hopped on bikes and rode like wild men. I couldn't believe Finn could work that out; when I say he was bent, I mean he was completely bent in half. He and the spunky four-year-old Garrett rode like champs.

We had these boys for about ten weeks as a result of drugs and neglect. Nothing was off limits as to what they would talk about. You never knew what would come out of their mouths. Total inappropriateness would shock us so badly that we either couldn't speak, or we couldn't get control of the laughter that would erupt. Their teachers loved them, and our family, church, and friends wrapped around them. They were the best-dressed kids around after a few weeks in our home. I had never seen so many wonderful hand-me-downs. Their time with us propelled me to start a foster closet at our church. It is still up and running today serving about forty foster children per year plus the ones that come through our home regularly. It has been a huge blessing and has allowed me to walk in my attic again.

During the boys' time with us, I had to do a maternity leave for the guidance counselor who had taken over when I had retired. Both boys were at the school where I was working, so it worked out well. Devonta was also placed with us during this time, and don't forget the original four. Then, Finn got the flu, and I had never seen a child that sick. I worried that he may die. Because of his physical problems, the illnesses took a harder toll on his body. I had to carry him from the chair in the den where his body lay lifeless for five days, to the bathroom, and to the bed. He could barely move. He scarcely ate or drank. Every day I was either taking him to the doctor or calling the nurse on call. I was so worried. After about a week, he began to gain strength and get back to himself. I was exhausted, and my husband had reached his breaking point. I will get to that in a minute.

My pediatrician had agreed to see the children even though he wasn't taking new patients anymore, and he probably usually didn't accept their state benefits. He is truly amazing, and I have always felt so blessed that he was my children's pediatrician and now my foster children's. I knew they would get the best care, which they deserved and needed. He took a personal interest in Finn and really got the ball moving on getting him some help and relief for his back, which he should have had years earlier. However, as luck would have it, right when we had our first appointment scheduled with a specialist, the boys were placed with a family member. I prayed that they would receive better care than their previous family member. I had a hard time trusting that would happen, but I didn't have a choice. Reunification was the goal, and that is what ensued.

Because we live in a small town, and everyone knows everyone, I was able to hear how the boys were doing occasionally. It was about four and half years later before Finn got the surgery that he needed, and he was in the hospital for most of the school year. We went to see him once, and he had not changed much at all—still winning hearts and spunky as ever! His "broken" made him all the better because if we have never been broken, we don't appreciate being whole. Five months later I got word that this precious child had died in his sleep due to complications. My daughter and I went to his funeral, where the pastor spoke of how this little boy brought so much joy and light to their small church. He had continued to be full of mischief and spontaneity that had made the church wrap around and love this child as we had. As the pastor spoke, I remembered the call I had made when the boys had left our home. I had felt God's gentle nudging to call the church and tell them of the two boys living in their community that would need to be surrounded. This sweet pastor had followed up on my call, and for the next six years he picked those boys up and got them to church on the church van. During this time and because of the relationship they formed, the pastor was able to have many discussions with Finn about Jesus and His love for His people. Sweet Finn knew Jesus, and I know that I will see him on the other side one day. We may never know why God is asking us to do certain things. We don't know why some children suffer and some die too early. We may not get to know this side of heaven. We just need to trust and obey those gentle nudges.

Of no fault of their own, the time the boys were with us was too busy. My husband and I were pulled apart trying to make everything happen. We had two children playing high school soccer, two more playing rec soccer, one doing college soccer, three foster children with a variety of needs, and both of us working full time, and we just got too busy. We took our eyes off Jesus. Time alone with just the two of us and time with the Lord were the first two things that we let go of to make space for all the other. We both went down and needed help. My pastor sent us to someone who we could talk to without our entire town knowing what was going on. I still worked part time for the church, and I just didn't want people to know how hard this all was for our family. Did you know that if you work at the church you should have it all together? It is a lot of pressure, and I felt it every time a child messed up and in my marriage struggles. I guess I needed the glass walls to stay somewhat blurred to make it look like things were better than they were. Why was it so hard? I mean God had called us to this place. Should it be this hard? Were we wrong? Are we messing it all up?

Well, we went to a marriage counselor. The counselor we saw gave us one bit of such simple advice, but it has stuck with us and changed our perspective. He told us to look around the room at all the objects in his office. Then, he wanted us to stare at the light in the room for a while. He then told us to try to notice the things around the room as you keep your eyes on the light. The objects in the room were different. The light was the main object, and then the other stuff just sort of didn't seem so big anymore. He compared this to life with a relationship with God at the center. He said when you keep your eyes on God, the things that are surrounding us fall into place around Him. They don't take over as the center of our lives when we keep our eyes focused on Him. It made sense to both of us, and it changed our outlook.

Like only God can do, He brought us back stronger than ever. Our relationship was stronger and more intentional than it had been before. It was good! Like Finn, we experienced brokenness and came back richer and more appreciative of our newfound wholeness in our relationship. Another illustration we focused on during this time is one I like to think of now too. Picture the cross in your mind. Look at the vertical beam. That is our relationship with God. He is pouring into us as we look up to Him, keeping our eyes on Him all the time. Then the overflow of that love relationship is what overflows from the horizontal beam to all those surrounding us. Our horizontal relationships suffer when we aren't strong with the Father in our vertical relationship.

Don't abandon your first love. Keep Him first, and all the others will fall into place. Our God is a jealous God, and He desires first place in your life. He knows this is what is best for all of us, and He *will* do whatever it takes to get our attention.

> *But I have this against you, that you have abandoned the love you had at first. Remember, therefore from where you have fallen; repent, and do the works you did at first. If not, I will come to you and remove your lampstand from its place, unless you repent. (Revelation 2:4–5)*

CHAPTER 5

IT TAKES A VILLAGE

See, I am sending an angel ahead of you
to guard you along the way and to bring
you to the place I have prepared.
—Exodus 23:20

After some recovery time when Devonta left, we did some respite care for other foster parents. One of the respites was an infant whose foster mom was having surgery. He was such a good baby, and we loved him, but after a couple of weeks we knew we should stick to a little older child with more independence. I was delighted when his foster mom was well and came to pick him up. I am learning that because I say yes to some things doesn't mean I have to say yes to everything.

We eventually got a call for a sibling group. The brother was in fourth grade and the sister was in second grade. They had been homeless for a while; mom was an addict, and dad wasn't around. We said yes, and they showed up on our front doorstep late one evening.

I will call these children James and Hazel. They ended up staying in our home for almost a year. They vacationed with us, played sports in our community, were invited to parties, received tutoring, accepted Jesus and were baptized in our church, and blended into our family. The resiliency I see in these children and most of the others is mind-boggling. They slipped into the places of our hearts and made a room for themselves.

When they first came to us, I spoke with their previous school counselor and teachers. My heart was touched by the ways these school personnel had given themselves to these children. They had gone over and above to try to help this family. It personifies what so many in the world of education do that goes unnoticed. They had filled in so many gaps and worked and worried so hard for these children to keep them out of the system and, more specifically, foster care. When they gave up and called DSS as a last resort, it hurt them to the core. But God had plans for these children, and His plans were unfolding. In my eyes, the teachers were angels God had placed around them for a time. Also, before they came into foster care, the school had placed them in an after-school homework center at a church across the street. There they received a snack, help with homework, activities, and a hot supper. The best part of the after-school program was that they assigned mentors for each of the children. James and Hazel were appointed a husband and wife pair. They would come and eat with the children, help with homework, and just check in with them weekly. Again, angels were placed around them. Six years later this couple still mentors James and Hazel. They take them places, provide for them, and even keep them occasionally for weekends.

One thing I want to mention here is that all the children, except for one, who have been placed in our home have been brought into foster care due to drug abuse by a parent. A large percent of these have been mothers, and then eventually the dads or grandparents get them back, and mom goes to jail or continues in her self-destructive lifestyle. James and Hazel's mom is an addict. She never accepted responsibility for her mistakes; she went in and out of jail and never made necessary life changes. When I met her at a monthly visit a few months into the children being with us, she refused to look at me and did not speak. She turned her back on me. I was a little ticked and a lot confused. How do you not ask this strange lady keeping your kids how they are doing, do they need anything, are they behaving, or here's a novel thought … what about a "thank-you"? Through the years I have noticed that parents who accept responsibility and make necessary changes will make it. Those who won't, don't. What a prophetic thought for our young parents raising children. Teach them *responsibility* for their actions, or they will never be successful contributors to society.

On the other hand, the maternal grandfather was working to get the children. He is on a low income, eighth-grade educated, sober alcoholic, and teachable. He was willing to do what he had to do, listen to advice, accept help, and be responsible. Another angel surrounding these children.

The children were with us eleven months before we had to plan another farewell party. My family supports us so much with each child who comes into our home. We could not make it without them. My niece and Hazel had become best friends.

She went on vacations with them and stayed with them a lot. James had made friends and had them over to play regularly. Now it was time to start over. Our church members, family, teachers, and friends came to the party. They brought gift cards for restaurants and notes of encouragement and love to these children to bless them as they started the next chapter in their lives. As each child left our house, I would make a scrapbook for him or her to keep. It was a therapeutic healing process for me, I think, and they loved them! I put all their cards, gift cards, and pictures in the scrapbooks and documented all the events that they had experienced in the past year. I didn't want it to be forgotten or a "lost" year of their development. I was a little apprehensive about all their needs being met in grandfather's home but trusted that God would keep providing for these children as had been so evidently shown.

We could meet the caseworker at grandfather's house to drop the children off. It was a sweet time, and grandfather was so accommodating, appreciative, and willing to do whatever to make this work. He wanted my advice about home and school and was very receptive to us maintaining a relationship with the children. He gave us his phone number, and he took mine, and a coparenting system was created. Again, God at work!

When I talked to him the following week, he reported that their mom had broken into the house and stolen all of their gift cards. It was hundreds of dollars' worth. He was furious; I was flabbergasted, and I don't even want to imagine what mark that left on her children forever. It is heartbreaking.

For the past six years the co-parenting has been working. "Papa" has had the same job for thirtyish years. He believes in hard work. When he misses a day though, he doesn't get paid. He has had a lot of health issues that have caused him to miss work continuously this last year. Their budget is tight and days without work devastate the already tight budget. So I help as much as possible though we are about forty-five minutes away. I am the school contact, take the children to doctor's appointments (Have I said how awesome my pediatrician is? He still sees them!), get them one or two weekends a month, did the braces thing, and whatever else is needed.

My brother's family still does a lot with them also. Their mentors get them and do things with them, too. A village is surrounding them, and I point this out to them as much as possible. I am not sure they get it yet, but I pray one day they will look back and see the mighty ways God put people in their lives at the right time to protect them and guide them. I pray it changes generations to come because their real life is still not ideal. Life at their home is still traumatic. I want to bang my head against the wall much of the time as I deal with schools that don't go over and above, and family members that I have to hide the children's money from and that cause me to check all of their medicine in with the school because they would steal it if it were at home. The children's academic work is regressing; it seems cognitive development has been dramatically slowed due to all the traumatic factors, and their behaviors can be trying. Things like this make me doubt the worth of the effort that we are giving, but I have not felt God release us of the responsibility of these precious children. I will keep on until I feel God moving me differently. I have needed to be continually reminded that we may not see the fruits of our labor on this side of eternity. If we build our lives around material things that can be seen, we will see progress, and some get great satisfaction for this momentary gain. However, when we are building spiritually for eternity, the progress is not as visible many times and can get quite frustrating. I encourage you to press on if you are in a similar situation where you are just getting weary of the work that seems to be going nowhere. God is not finished! He has shown Himself faithful to His children thus far, and I am trusting that He will continue until the day He calls us home.

> *He will wipe every tear from their eyes, and death shall be no more, neither shall there be mourning, nor crying, nor pain anymore, for the former things have passed away. Behold, I am making all things new. (Revelation 21:4–5)*

CHAPTER 6
WHAT JUST HAPPENED?

*He heals the brokenhearted and binds up
their wounds. He counts the number of
the stars; He calls them by name.
—Psalm 147:3–4*

Again, we took a long break, just doing a few respite care placements. One evening on our way to a soccer game, I got a phone call about four children who needed care for *the night*. We were rushing around; my husband got home right as we were leaving. We jumped in the car and took off to the game. After the game I said something like, "Oh, yeah, we are meeting DSS here to keep some kids for the night." By this time, two of our biological children were in college, one was a junior in high school and one was a freshman. All four of us still in the home were in the car. Then, we pile in four little people. They were eight, five, three, and ten months. I wish I could tell you their real names because it would give you insight into what just happened. I will call them Kiki, Lacey, Malcom, and Prince. Again, switching children in a parking lot at night. Can you imagine? The children move into the car, and our lives are totally disrupted. My husband is not having fun. My two kids are laughing like crazy and getting acquainted with the children. I am moving back and forth between hysteria and type A crazy lady. They came with *nothing*. No bottles, no diapers, no clothes, nothing. The baby is crying. My husband is looking at me like he could really kill me right now. I can't stop laughing out loud inadvertently. I make one phone call. *Help!* I talk to a young mother; she makes some calls, and twenty minutes later she meets me at our house with everything we need. We all work steady to get them bathed, fed, and in the bed. Then we collapse thinking we will be up soon, but praise God again, no one woke up all night!

These children were wounded. They had been hurt and mishandled worse than any children who had been through our house. I could not let them go to other foster homes. I knew it was important for these to be kept together right now. Our one night turned into two weeks of complete chaos. I may never know how all of this affects my own children, but I do pray that it is for their good more so than the bad. That what they are experiencing propels them to a place beyond themselves, free of fear of loving and losing, understanding that living a life for God looks different, and it is okay. They love and serve these children only to let them go to who knows where. It is hard. My children are strong, and I am so proud of each of them. There is no way I could have done this group without them and my mom. It was all hands on deck! There was more emotional instability than the entire child and adolescent wing at the psychiatric hospital where I taught my first year as a teacher.

There were tears, temper tantrums, screaming, cussing (a lot), and pent-up fears and hurts coming out all sorts of ways. One sweet nursery worker at our church would come to me crying on several occasions because the three-year-old had called her bad names and literally cussed her out. It was so hard not to take it personally. The kindergarten teacher called me in tears over a story Lacey had shared—a story of things that had happened to her that could leave her broken and victimized forever. They all were fighting their demons, and my heart and my family's hearts were broken for these children. We poured Jesus into them. We read Bible stories; we talked and talked; we prayed over hurts; we modeled the Father's love and forgiveness over and over. Again, I just pray it was enough and trust that God can take the smallest seeds and do incredible things. I pray for these children often and wonder how they are doing. They came in like a whirlwind and left much the same way. They didn't want to go. They were only with us two weeks before arrangements were made for all but Prince to go to different family members. They kicked and screamed and cried to stay with us. My mama and daughter were there to love them bye and help me load them all up. We were all a mess! It was the most traumatic scene I have experienced. The seasoned caseworker couldn't get over it and really didn't know what to do. They left us screaming and crying, and it is forever ingrained in my mind. This is another instance where I will never know the purpose of their brief stay in our home until I see the Father. Again, I pray and trust it was for His good.

Each night we would all read to the children and say prayers with them. It took us all working together to make bedtime a success. Then my younger daughter and I would fight over who got to put Prince to bed. As we would sing and pray over him, he would just wrap around your neck and hold on for dear life. It felt like his very life was seeping into mine, and I think my daughter felt it too. It was both endearing and heartbreaking at the same time. It was a glimpse of his need for love and affection. He needed someone to hold on to. We fell in love hard with this baby. It was a fierce love born from protection and need. It overtook me in unexpected ways. I tried to share him with others, but I didn't want to. I was a baby hog! My daughter fought for bedtime duty at night, because I got to get him out of bed in the mornings and at naptime and receive the same sweet hugs. Bath time, feeding him, reading to him, playing with him … every second with him was a special gift from God.

He was such an unexpected joy! About a week into the children's stay with us, I was putting Prince to bed, and I will never forget I heard the voice of God tell me that Prince would be staying longer than the other siblings and that He had big plans for him. As I would hold him and pray over him, I would think of Martin Luther King or other black men of greatness and could feel God assuring me this child would be great. I was not one bit surprised when DSS told me they didn't know his father and couldn't find family for him yet. They needed him to stay with us for a time longer. I was not surprised. I also will not be surprised one day when I read his name in the paper or hear of him doing something great! God has a purpose for this child. He has promised.

> *For I know the plans I have for you declares the Lord, plans to prosper you and not to harm you, plans to give you a hope and a future. (Jeremiah 29:11)*

We had him for four months. Everyone who came into contact with him fell in love with him. Several parents decided to foster because of him. He changed us all for the better.

When I say I grieved this baby leaving, I mean I grieved. I still cry at the mention of his name, and as I type these thoughts about him, I feel the pain of the heartbreak all over again. He took a piece of my heart with him. The grieving is a sticky situation because a lot of people feel like you have asked for it by putting yourself out there. I mean, I choose to be a foster parent. Or that because you knew they would be leaving, you should have been prepared. I feel like talking about it just gets on people's nerves and makes them judge or doubt our decision to foster. I am thankful God has placed a couple of people around me that let me grieve and see my pain.

So this brings me to my pet peeve. So many people say they could not foster because they would just get too attached. Well,

I just don't know what to say to that. Do they think we don't get attached? Do they think my heart doesn't hurt? Do they think I am some callous, hard-hearted person? When people say that, I feel myself wanting to scream, "It does hurt!" There are other things I want to say, but as I am getting older, I am learning some of the art of self-control. Trust me, it hurts me, but does that mean we shouldn't do it? I found a quote by Jason Johnson that says, "Foster care means choosing the pain of great loss if it means a child has received the gain of a great love." I pray our great losses have been a great gain for these children. It really isn't about us anyway.

Now that I know the pain that came with this child and all the other children, do I wish we had not decided to foster? Do I wish we had said no when we were asked to keep them? Do I wish I had not have loved them with my whole heart? Absolutely not! I would not have wanted to miss any of this. These experiences with these children have enriched our family. They have given us insight and empathy and a heart for all of God's people—most of all for those broken and downtrodden. We would have missed so much if we had not followed God's plan to foster.

There are so many songs running through my head right now, but Garth Brooks's song "The Dance" is the loudest.

> *And now I'm glad I didn't know*
> *The way it all would end—the way it all would go.*
> *Our lives are better left to chance (we all know it's not chance); I could have missed the pain, but I'd of had to miss the dance.*

I want to live life in such a way that I don't miss one thing that God has for me. Missing His blessings and plans scares me more than any amount of hurt and failure could ever scare me.

CHAPTER 7

SISTERS OF THE HEART

*Whoever does God's will is my
brother and sister and mother.*
—Mark 3:35

Our next long-term children came walking in our front door late one night visibly shaken. They were stunning. The older one, Aisha, was seven years old and in second grade. She had the most beautiful chocolate skin and was the sort of beauty that would make people take a second look. The six-year-old, who we will call Marisa, earned the nickname Smiley right off the bat. She had light skin, beautiful blue eyes, and a constant smile even in her fearful state. She was in first grade. They looked like Disney princesses straight out of the movies. However, as with many of our children, we had been warned that they had lice in their hair. So, out came the "lice kit," and that process began.

When I say I hate lice, I mean *I hate* lice. It is pure trauma for everyone involved. When I was a guidance counselor at the primary school, I had dealings with it and learned how to check for it and how to treat it. My friends and I were blessed with it in our homes a few times when our children were young. If you have never been lucky enough to have to go through this process, you just can't understand the trauma. It takes hours and hours of treating and cleaning and pulling hair and crying. It is miserable. My pediatrician once said that there needed to be a support group for moms of children who had lice. That is the truth. Whenever new children come into our home, I immediately wash everything. I also treat for lice. It is protocol.

Well, this night I treated and worked some, but it was too much. When I say covered, I mean covered. The next morning, we took our first trip to the "lice doctor," where they charge you a small fortune, and you gladly pay it with the guarantee that they will terminate every last one of the pests. I have gotten to be quite the lice expert through the years. Friends call me anytime a louse is sighted at their home, and I go over and work my magic. I am not sure why God has given me this qualification, but I try to use it as a blessing to others.

Anyway, before we went to the lice doctor, we were sent to a drug testing center for a hair sample to be taken to see if the girls tested positive for drugs. This was like so many of our stories—a story of a mom with a drug addiction. She was also one of the moms who when I met her, she was looking to find fault in the caseworkers and us. She could only place blame on the system and everyone around her and never recognized her faults. She is also one of the parents that never said thank-you and is still in jail today. When we stay a victim, never accept responsibility, and have not received consequences for bad behavior throughout our lifetime, it is hard to be an adult who succeeds in society. I have seen it over and over with family members, in the schools, churches, and in the foster-care arena. Children need consequences for their behavior; whether the behavior is good or bad; they need to recognize that there are consequences. Parents, teach your children well. We are not their buddies. God has given us a job as parents. It is work. Raise these children to be strong adults. God gives us such great instructions in His word. Read this as you parent children to be great adults.

Most of the children who have come through our home have been neglected in so many ways, and educationally is at the top. They have all been behind at school except for these two girls. They were so naturally smart. They each tested "gifted and talented" and excelled academically, musically, and artistically. I was estatic that I had a break from the dreaded homework hell. I had even prayed before they came that maybe, just maybe, our next kids would not need so much academic help. Isn't it amazing how He cares for even our selfish needs? I was thankful!

Again, these girls were so easy to love. They were funny and cute even if they were a little overboard with the girl drama. They fit in at school and at church, and many loved them. My daughters bonded with them and were wonderful role models while the girls were here. They made videos, had dance parties and pillow fights, and did all the fun stuff that would have been uncool if they did it with me. The girls stayed about three months before they were placed with another family member. It was yet another colliding conflict of emotions as we all said goodbye. The children wanted to go to family but didn't want to leave us. We are all about reunification but hated to say goodbye and put the girls into an unknown situation. Here was another opportunity to grow in our faith. Yay!

We took a break for a couple of months to get through Christmas and a few family trips before we opened our home back up for a long-term placement. Right before Valentine's Day we got another sweet second-grader who we will call Caydence. She was beautiful and smart! I couldn't believe it! She had been in a foster home and was having trouble getting along with another child, so they moved her to us. She was terrified when they brought her to our house. She had such a look of fear that I just wanted to take her in my arms and hold her tight, but I quickly recognized the "fight or flight" protection wall she had in place. It hurt my heart to think of all she must have been experiencing and thinking as she walked into our house. I wanted to gather her up and hold her, but this little girl needed to have some space. She was going to be strong and didn't want any weakness to be visible. She was only seven years old and was now being moved to yet another foster home full of strangers. Caydence was a fighter. She had learned to fight for what she needed and wanted. Sometimes she did this inappropriately, but she was teachable, and we saw through her mask to all the vulnerability she was trying to cover. Again, we assured her she was safe, and we watched her begin to relax and flourish while she was here. The first night she was with us we discovered we knew her second-grade teacher from the school she was leaving, so we contacted her to tell her that Caydence was with us. We were all excited about the opportunity to stay in contact since this teacher's daughter and my daughter were on the same soccer team. We got to see her several times a week at soccer games, and she even did respite care for us once when we had to be out of town. To keep Caydence's village intact was important. It was such a blessing to have this relationship with her teacher present through her move to another home and school. Keeping as many members of a child's village together as possible is very beneficial. It makes that foundation stronger so that when they leave us, they are more confident and stable.

Well, we had Caydence a few days when we were sitting at the table making Valentines for her class, and we got a call. Aisha and Marisa were back in custody. They had tested positive for drugs again while living with the new family member. Again, I say; this is such a generational cycle! Sometimes it feels so hopeless to stop or make a difference with these families where drugs and dysfunction are their normal. Anyway, back to the story. We all decided that we didn't want the girls to have to adjust to another foster home, so we said, "Sure! We will take them." When they brought them to our house that night, it was like they had never been away. They were right at home, and they did not miss a beat. The only difference was that another little girl was in their room.

The next three months were crazy. We were the most multiculturally diverse family that we could be. We had triplets, it seemed, but one was African American, one was white, and one was Hispanic. They were "stop-and-stare" gorgeous! We were definitely noticed when we were brave enough to go off the farm.

Little girls were everywhere! They shared a double bunk bed set. They had more clothes to work with than a department store. People sent the most beautiful hand-me-downs, and we dressed them up as much as they would let us. Picking out outfits became such a stressor that I finally had to assign a theme for each day. There were dress alike days, legging days, jeans day, etc. We also learned that mornings were more likely to be a success if we laid out the outfits the night before, and no one was allowed to change her mind once the outfit was decided.

A Friendship Born from Pain, Formed from Love

They played dolls for hours. Dolls were all over the house, the yard, the car, and even the swimming pool. We were now a family of two teens at home, three little girls, and at least three baby dolls whenever we went anywhere. They swam constantly, played all over the farm, and fought like real sisters. The two second-graders were fairly hardheaded, and you had to pick your battles with them for sure. I never want to break a spirit because I feel God has equipped them for a purpose. It will benefit them as they grow and navigate through this life. They were strong young ladies with so much potential. I pray they stay focused on God the Father and use that hardheadedness to bring Him honor.

There were meltdowns, crying, tantrums, whining, bathroom issues, eating battles, and messes to clean, but through it all these girls developed a bond that has lasted through the years. They love each other so much, and it does my heart good to see how that relationship was formed from pain and grown from love.

After three months, right at the end of the school year, Marisa's dad completed the requirements for him to get custody of both girls. Though he was not the biological father of both girls, they both called him daddy, and through the years he has definitely proven that he is their daddy. He is not just a "baby daddy" but a real daddy, born not of blood but out of love, loyalty, responsibility, and honor for both of these girls equally.

On the day they left, Aisha wrote us the sweetest letter ever. I keep it framed and in sight to remind me of our calling and that God is using us to make a difference in the lives of these children. No matter how hard, it is worth it! Aisha gave me permission to share this letter. It is precious to me.

> I really loved staying with you.
> You played with me alot.
> When I was feeling blue you always were there.
> I mite come and visit you on the weekend.
> You were nice enough to take me in from DSS.
> You were always kind and sweet.
> You helped us when we painted the fort.
> You cooked for us at breakfast, lunch and Dinner.
> When I got hurt you always cared.
> You told us about the Lord.
> You took me to church.
> You took me to School when I needed to get smart.

Caydence was lost when the girls left. As much as they fought and got on each other's nerves, she missed them like crazy. Our house was too quiet. Thank goodness she had good friends at church, and our summer was full of activities. We immersed her in camps and summer school and vacations to keep her busy. Much to our delight, Aisha and Marisa's daddy let the girls come to visit some, and that helped so much.

That summer Caydence asked Jesus into her heart. We were all so excited! We talked to her grandmother who was trying to get custody, and she was delighted. Caydence was baptized at our church, and her daddy and maternal grandmother came to watch. Afterward, we all went out to eat and to celebrate. We had a great time being together, and another friendship was formed with a family so different from my own but with the same desire to see this child flourish and grow. Really, we all may look and think differently; we do things differently, but most of us just want the best for our children. Wouldn't it be awesome to be in a world where we looked past differences and just all worked together for the betterment of each other? Oh, yes, I think God says that somewhere ...

There are at least one hundred Bible verses on it. Here are two that stand out:

> *Let each of you look not only to his own interests, but also to the interests of others. (Philippians 2:4)*

> *With humility and gentleness, with patience, bearing with one another in love. (Ephesians 4:2)*

In September, Caydence's mother's mom and her dad, with whom she had never lived, secured joint custody of her. It is an unusual setup, but it is working for her good. In their home are grandma, step-grandfather, dad, Caydence's older brother from a different father, a baby brother with a different father, and now a little sister. There are also four other half siblings who are with their own dad or have been adopted by foster parents. I must be honest when I say that I have zero respect for this mom. She has only been hateful to me, and I have watched her hurt Caydence with her words and her actions of rejection and nonchalance. She has mental issues and drug issues that society turns its head from in fear of infringing on her rights. I want to talk about the rights of others who she has infringed upon. She has eight children from seven different men. All but one has tested positive for drugs at birth; the children are removed from her custody at birth. She refuses to get on birth control or get fixed. We push for people to neuter/spay their animals but don't seem to care about the children born into these situations. Taxpayers are paying an estimated $100,000 per child until their eighteenth birthday. These children will battle abandonment, neglect, and all the issues surrounding this unhealthy mom for the rest of their lives. Where are their rights? Where are the taxpayers' rights? She is not the only one; there are plenty of other women doing this that I have been made aware of during the fostering experience. They don't get prenatal care; they don't care about their children, and they have them and walk away knowing someone will clean up their mess, and they have no responsibility whatsoever. This is not okay. I do not understand the silence with this issue and why our society is so afraid to address it.

Anyway, back to the story. As our children leave our home, I always plan some sort of farewell event just to celebrate them and acknowledge their time with us. How long they were with us and the relationships they formed determine what we do as a celebration. Sometimes it is just something with our family, sometimes a few friends, and sometimes a *big* party. For Caydence I wanted to do a small celebration at church with her church friends since she had been there for seven months. It would be good for her and for our church family/children to get to say goodbye as they have all invested in each other in some way. Well, on the night we had planned the church event, she inadvertently was forgotten. Her feelings were hurt, and so were mine. I tried to be positive, reminding both of us that we were having a real party that weekend for family and friends to say goodbye. However, it reminded me that unless you are in the trenches, you just don't understand the sacrifice and the opportunity these children represent. They are easily overlooked because it is easier to do that than to notice all their hurt and pain. As a foster parent their pain becomes my pain, and their hurt feelings resonate in my soul just like my own children's do. Perhaps I don't do a great job of making others aware of the opportunities and needs of these children. Most people don't feel called to foster. However, so much can be done to support fostering. Our friends have done some neat things that really made a difference for us. I will include some ideas here:

1. First, no one can touch what my parents and brother's family have done to support us with meals, visits, respite care, play dates, calls, words of affirmation, gifts, and so much more. Some people think not just anyone can babysit or keep these children. That is not true. Anyone that I would allow my children to visit or stay with can have these children over too.
2. I mentioned that I started a foster closet at our church. That has been a huge help for me and many other foster families in our community. Our church members have stocked it, and now some of the ladies keep it organized and functional.
3. When we first started fostering, a few people brought a meal when we got a new placement. That was a huge help.
4. Hand-me-downs!
5. Some of our youth have helped with tutoring. This is a *huge* need.
6. One of our friends invites our family over for dinner when we get a new placement. This gives them an opportunity to get to know the children and for the child to see another family's dynamics.
7. We have a photographer at our church who does a photo shoot for free of the children that come through our home.

A lot of times this is the only "real" picture the children have of themselves.

8. When a child is invited to a party or over for a play date or on a trip to the movies, it is a *big* deal. It is an opportunity that our own children take for granted but impacts these children in such positive ways.
9. Trust them with responsibilities. One friend asked one of my teens to babysit, and I promise she walked with her head higher because of it. She did an awesome job too! Some of the boys have been given yard work chores or other jobs, and it has created in them a sense of pride and self-worth that someone would trust them to do a job and pay them for their efforts.
10. Financial assistance can be impactful with summer camps, church events, dance classes, tennis lessons, or whatever. One to five extra children in the home add up fast and can become a financial burden to a family in a hurry.
11. Calls and letters of encouragement are a treasure. Or a genuine conversation where the needs of our family and the foster child are truly a concern.

We need more foster families! We are ordinary. Nothing special. We are just regular people like you doing what God has called us to do. We are only equipped because of Him. If you just can't, then please consider what you could do to come along beside them and help. How could you use your gifts to provide for the orphans in your area?

I saw the following tidbit online and think it is appropriate for here. Don't let fear stop you from doing what God is calling you to do.

> *God found Gideon in a hole.*
> *He found Joseph in prison.*
> *He found Daniel in a lion's den.*
>
> *He has a curious habit of showing up*
> *In the midst of trouble, not the absence.*
> *Where the world sees failure,*
> *God sees future.*
>
> *Next time you feel unqualified to be*
> *Used by God remember this, He tends*
> *To recruit from the pit, not the pedestal.*

Wow! We are all unqualified, but He isn't. He takes us from our weakness, so we recognize His strength. He is the Hero!

It is always hard to let the children go when they leave. It is a step of faith that God is in control, and He goes before them wherever they are headed. When it was time for Caydence to go home, the children and were allowed to take her home and help settle her in. She and my older daughter had gotten very close and were best of friends. She came home from college and went with me and my youngest two to unpack her and see where she would be living. Her home is small, and glimpses of poverty are visible. However, it was neat and clean, and most of all, the family was delighted to have her with them. It was a win as the goal of reunification was met in a healthy, creative manner. On a side note, I went back to the house another time with Aisha and Marisa for Caydence's birthday party. A lot of her family was there including mom. Mom texted some bad words on her phone for me and held them so that I could see them clearly. It was a welcoming gesture that confirmed my lack of enthusiasm for her mothering skills. (Insert sarcasm.) Caydence still must be subjected to her, which makes me have to continuously keep God in the seat of control. He loves these people more than me, and He's got them.

Our family has been very blessed in that we get all three of the girls about every other month or so for the weekend. We have summer camps at our house where we play and do tons of activities. They always just fit right back together like no time has passed. They have been to each other's birthday parties, they still go to our church camp together, they Facetime each other, and now that they are getting a little older, they have sleepovers at each other's houses. The older two are about to start middle school. Conversations and activities have changed, but the dialogue is always open and honest and real. We always talk about who Jesus is to them and how they are living out being a Christian at home and at school. It is a joy to be a part of the lives of these young women who were taken from a life full of drugs and neglect and watch them flourish in an environment of hope and love. I am their family's biggest cheerleader! I am so proud of the job they are doing! These families listen to advice, aren't afraid of work, and accept responsibility. They are going to make it. Thanks be to God!

CHAPTER 8

DJJ OR US

*I sought the Lord, and he answered me
and delivered me from all my fears.*
—*Psalm 34:4*

Hmmm ... Are you ever just overwhelmed by the opportunity that God has put in your path? Sometimes when I am riding down the road or walking through the woods at home, or I have just experienced a "God sighting," I have the desire to just hit my knees because of the greatness of the Lord. I am overcome and overwhelmed that He has blessed me in such magnitude, overwhelmed that He chooses to use me for His good purpose. Why me, Lord? I am perhaps the most average person you could ever meet. Why would the God of the universe choose to use me? Well, He uses us when we are willing. We are not the independent variable; He is. We are dependent and usable only because of Him. I don't know why me, but I know He loves me, and I trust Him, and I want to follow Him with my whole heart. I think about Exodus 33:15 quite often as I go into a different situation. I beg God, as Moses did: "If your Presence does not go with us, do not send us up from here."

I don't want to go anywhere that God is not sending me, walking ahead of me, preparing the way. I have plenty of experience going my own way, and the consequences of that have not been favorable. A new idea was forming, and I was very apprehensive about it. I sure didn't want to go this route unless God was going ahead of us, preparing the way.

Once the girls left, and we took a break to get one more child graduated from high school, the idea of taking in teenagers began to take shape. I barely like my own teenagers. I only worked with children in the church and schools. I fear them, so I balked at this from the beginning. However, parts of it began to make sense. Our only biological child left at home now was in high school, so it might be easier to try older children with more of the same interests as him. Not everyone wants teens, so we knew a need existed for foster homes for them. Finally, breaking free of the chains of fear, we took the leap. Teens it would be.

Well, one evening we received a call about a fourteen-year-old boy that we will call Usey. The placement worker explained the problem that had gotten this child removed from his home and told us they were torn between placing him with the Department of Juvenile Justice or in foster care. Well, that gave me a warm, fuzzy feeling for our first foster teen placement. I was petrified! However, he, just like the younger children who we had gotten before, came into our home vulnerable, hurt, and alone. We welcomed him, showed him his room, told him he was safe with us, and let him go to bed with the promise of talking things out the next day. The next day we gave him a tour of the farm and helped him to get his bearings. The outdoors and animals were like salve to his soul. He became a natural on the farm and showed great responsibility. We also started working on his school priorities. Since he was in high school, a lot of collaborating had to be done to be sure credits would transfer and classes were offered that he needed. He was smart but had changed schools so often that he had fallen behind. We worked hard on making school a success while he was with us.

As you have noticed, church is a big part of our lives. We are there pretty much every time the doors open. Well, we soon learned that Usey had never been to church before. Not even once. I couldn't believe it! I found it hard to fathom that someone born in America had never been to church. I was overcome with the magnitude of responsibility that came with this child that God had placed in our home. There was a ton of dialogue about his family's beliefs versus ours. We never pushed him but felt God had placed him with us for a purpose. We shared the gospel with him and read the Bible stories that he had never heard before. It was so interesting reading these stories with a teen with no prior knowledge. He was not afraid to ask questions and caused us to dig deeper into the word so that we could answer his questions. He loved our church and the friends he made there. My nephew was his age, and he took him under his wing and made life at a new high school much easier. He and his friends also included him at youth events. It was a very positive experience for Usey. A bond was formed between him and my son that was so healthy and good for Usey to experience during this time. Since the heartbreak of Devonta, I will say that our youngest did not put himself on the line again. That hurt was hard, and he has not been willing to go all in again. However, he and Usey got along great, and in the friendship, Usey found an awesome role model. My son recognized that Usey was with us for a purpose, and he took his role as a reflection of Christ very seriously. I was and am so proud of his desire for Usey to know the Lord and the leadership he took on. Again, it was a win-win for both sides with God loving and growing both of these boys.

As a foster parent our goal is for reunification. I pray for the families; I don't tear down parents in front of their children, and I encourage communication during the children's time with us whenever possible. I've had our foster children's families to celebrations and gone to theirs. I have been blessed with the best family ever, and I want that for these children that I love. I want their family to succeed. Well, with Usey, I couldn't wrap my brain around his situation, so my husband and I took an entire day to go to his court hearing. We only do this if there is a question about the goal. Well, when we got there, we were treated like the black sheep of the family. The caseworker did not speak to us. She did not try to introduce us to the family or give us any voice at all. When I walked out of the courthouse that day, I was *furious*! My husband had to literally hold me from going back in and sharing my frustration with each of them. I did write a letter and met with the caseworker's supervisor, which made me feel a little better, but I had definitely gotten a glimpse of where the foster parents fit in the hierarchy in the eyes of the powers that be. We are at the bottom of the ladder with no voice and no consideration. I will never be able to wrap my mind around that. I mean, who do they think gets to know these children the best and hear the horrid details of their lives? Good grief, caseworkers are with them one hour a month at most. We are the ones getting all of the details, the ones hearing their cries, and loving the unlovable. The system doesn't know what it is missing by not letting foster parents have a voice.

Usey was only with us one month, but he called one day about a week after he had moved home and was so excited to tell me that his entire family had gone to church together. It was a definite praise report! I count it a *win*! Even if they only went a few times, seeds were planted, and God can take any effort and make it bigger than we can imagine.

He was a blessing to have in our home, and a great first attempt with a teen. We have seen him on several occasions, been to his home, and talk to him regularly via text or phone. I feel like we will always connect with Usey, and he will forever be a part of our lives. God confirmed that He had my back; all I needed to do was to say yes. Don't let fear and doubt stop you from what God is calling you to do.

> *Jesus looked at them and said, "With man this is impossible, but with God all things are possible." (Matthew 19:26)*

CHAPTER 9

STRANDED

*"Turn to me and be gracious to me, for I am
lonely and afflicted."* Psalm 25:16 NIV

Not long after Usey went home we got another call about two teenage sisters. Their mom had abandoned them at some storage buildings when they told her she shouldn't be driving under the influence. From the beginning you could tell that the older sister, Viola, was the mother of the group. She was wise beyond her years. Mom was an illegal immigrant, which along with her act of abandonment, sent her to jail. Again, drugs were involved. Do you notice the common thread in most of these cases of child removal? Drugs are the number one culprit. I also have seen a link to poverty, an I-am-not-responsible attitude, and lack of a desire for a job. Many of the parents we have seen are completely content receiving government assistance. Work ethic and responsibility are things of the past for many of these families. Fostering is an opportunity to show the benefits of being independent and self-sufficient.

Breaking this cycle seems even harder because we are now enforcing these traits in our school system with a lack of discipline and accountability. The child who puts forth no effort and takes away the rights of his fellow classmates by continuously causing a disturbance in class is handed a diploma just to get the graduation numbers higher. The child that has worked his tail off for twelve years gets the same diploma. We are teaching them they don't have to work or be responsible. Society will just keep carrying you through. A lot of schools now won't even give a child a zero for incomplete work. They get a fifty for doing nothing. We are teaching them that they still get something even if they put forth no effort. This is not real life. It is unrealistic to let them think their whole life will be full of people compensating for their lack of effort. It is why our welfare system is in such a mess. We are teaching our next generation to expect something for nothing. When children aren't given discipline and responsibility and consequences for their actions, they grow up to be adults with the same characteristics.

These girls were not the problem. We were amazed at their ability to speak both English and Spanish fluently. They were so smart in many ways but very behind in school because of the many days they had been absent to stay home and take care of mom. They felt so much responsibility for her. It was heartbreaking to hear their stories and see how especially Viola had been robbed of a childhood. She had been the "parent" from a very early age. Taking care of her mom and her younger sister were her responsibility. At our house I tried to get her to stop and have some fun. Turns out, it was a habit too hard to break.

These girls were beautiful and grounded beyond belief. God had placed a guardian angel in their lives several years earlier in one of Viola's friend's mom. She had spent a lot of time helping the girls and wanted them as part of her family. She and her entire family rallied together in a heartwarming show of solidity to get the girls. The friend's mom, her mom, and all the mom's children came to meetings, got their houses in order, and completed every paper needed. They called to talk to the girls each day. I talked to her also and a bond of camaraderie was formed. We were all working together for the good of these girls. They were precious treasures that God had entrusted us with for this time. What an honor to be part of His plan again. I just can't get over how He was using us just because we said yes to His plan. I get saddened when I think of the times I haven't said yes. Think of all the blessings we miss when we don't take that leap of faith and follow Him when He calls. I heard a story once about a man who went to heaven. He was welcomed by Saint Peter at the gates and told he could do whatever he wanted to in heaven except look behind this one door. Well, of course the man wanted to know what was behind the closed door. We all want that one thing we can't have, right? Saint Peter said it would only make him sad if he looked in there, and there is no sadness in heaven. The man begged and finally Saint Peter relented. When they opened the door, it was full of all the blessings the man had missed by ignoring what God had called him to or blessings he missed by not asking for them in a *big* way and with *faith*. I know this is not true, but it does make me think. God wants to bless us beyond measure. Don't limit His blessings!

> *And God is able to bless you abundantly, so that in all things at all times, having all that you need, you will abound in every good work. (2 Corinthians 9:8)*

So we kept the girls for about four weeks while the friend's mom completed all of the legalities. It was an honor to keep them and a true blessing to our family. My girls, my mom, and I loved them and had a fast-growing relationship with them. They did dance videos, shopped, cooked some wonderful Hispanic foods for us, and introduced us to their culture. We all improved in some areas of the Spanish language. They were with us in November, so during their time they helped us put together boxes for Samaritan's Purse. These are shoebox-sized boxes that you can pack up for children in other countries that may not get Christmas gifts. It is a small way to show love for those that we may never know. I didn't think much about it, but the next Thanksgiving they sent us pictures of them completing boxes with their new family. My heart soared. Foster care can be a thankless job, and this was a gift to me. Maybe we were making a difference somewhere for God's glory. Maybe they would remember things that would make a difference for good.

When they left, we were able to see them a few times and even went to Viola's high school graduation and Weezie's class beauty pageant, which she won! I expect to hear good things from these young ladies, and again I stand amazed that we could be a part of their lives. I am beginning to like teenagers.

CHAPTER 10
PURPLE WEAVE AND SCABIES!

*As we look not to the things that are seen
but to the things that are unseen.
For the things that are seen are transient, but
the things that are unseen are eternal.*
—2 Corinthians 4:18

When you get a call for a child, the DSS placement worker will share what he or she knows about the circumstances that led to removal of the child from the home. The workers don't usually know very much, but I have gotten the heads-up about lice or siblings or a few other things. This time they wanted to be sure I knew all the children had scabies and would I be okay with that. Well, I had to look that up. I had never had dealings with scabies before, but I figured it couldn't be worse than lice. Have I said how much I loathe lice? All four of the children had already been placed in separate foster homes except for the oldest. She was fourteen years old. We decided we could take her, and for some reason, thought it would be for about four to six weeks. I guess we thought that because the other teens had only been for that amount of time. Never try to second guess the system. Anyway, it has been fifteen months, and we still have her as I type this out.

We will call this child Zenna. She walked in the door, and my heart stopped. Wait a minute, everything in me screamed! No way, not me. I wanted to back out of the plan. She was taller than me, built like a Victoria's Secret model, and a long purple weave covered her head. *Oh Lord, here we go*, I thought. *This is going to be bad. This is the teen I have been dreading!* Well, let this be a lesson for us all. Don't ever judge a person by his or her looks or a book by its cover. This child was/is precious and possibly the easiest foster we have had in our home over a longer time. We did respite care for one of her brothers and her sister a couple of times while Zenna was with us. Not much sibling bonding was present, but the same weaknesses were evident, letting me know that they had all been neglected equally. Also, I got the easiest sibling! God knows what I can handle.

Her first day with me is worth mentioning, and I don't think she will mind. We laugh about it quite often. During this time, I was teaching a form of sex education in the middle schools. She could not go to her school that first day because they needed to get her records in order. She had to go to work with me and sit in sex ed all day. She was a trooper, and it helped us reach a new level of rapport quickly. She fits the mold with the reason she was removed from her home. She has been neglected academically and socially. She did not bring many life experiences to the table. I am not sure what her family did because she knew nothing about anything. While she has been with us, she has experienced sleepovers, youth trips, birthday parties, snow skiing, boating on the lake and the ocean, tubing, horseback riding, being part of a tennis team and a track team, dance, A/B honor roll, first-time beach trips, learning to swim, a part-time job, concerts, plays, musicals, farm life, babysitting, bike riding, shopping trips, chores, family dinner time, and so many more things that she had never before experienced. We take these things for granted and assume most Americans get these opportunities. Well, plenty of children are sitting in homes where adults are not taking an interest in them. They think this is all there is. Without life experiences, how can they realize what all is out there for them?

How can they want more? How can they be more? How can they even test well because they have no idea what half of the stories or dialogue they are reading about relates to? It is mind-boggling that children in our area are caught in so much poverty and a state of backwardness. Closing a blind eye to the situations all around you is not okay. Even if you don't feel called to foster, there are so many mentoring opportunities that could change a life.

Zenna has experienced success. She lives out a life as a Christian and is very self-assured in her beliefs. Her friend group while with our family has been exceptional. I must give a shout-out to my niece again. She has reached out with acceptance and grace and pulled Zenna into her friend group. These precious girls have surrounded her with Jesus. They include her in parties and Bible studies and have helped her see a different way of life—a life of support and encouragement, one of families where mamas and daddies are present, and a life that recognizes the importance of working hard in school and in life. Through it all she rises above, and I have no doubt she will be different than what she has been subjected to in her life. Hopefully, the chain of drugs and poverty and laziness will be stopped. She will go home soon, and I am praying that she stands strong and that God keeps His hand on her and uses her to make a difference in generations! I have no doubt He can do that through her. She is remarkable, and we have been blessed to call her ours for over a year.

It seems she will go home in a month or two, but who knows? This is another hard part of fostering—the roller coaster ride, I call it. There are no clear-cut answers or timelines. I hate this part! It is like waiting to pull the Band-Aid off, and it is going so slowly. You know the pain that is coming, and you just want to rip it off and be done with it. It is the dread and fear because you have been here before. There is no way to avoid the pain that is coming, and that makes me crazy. I went to court last week for what was to be the last time. Plans were made, and the transition back to mom was supposed to start that weekend. Well, next thing we know the deal is off, and people who don't even know the children decide we will come back together in sixty days to look at the case again. Sixty days! Really? What a domino effect of hurt this was. It was like taking an eighteen-wheeler down a mountain road, and then suddenly there was a roadblock, and now you must turn that thing around right there and then. The case, as some call it, involves a huge number of people who must monitor and adjust. All the children and foster parents had come to terms with reunification. Tears had been shed, plans made, schools alerted, friends told, and foster siblings notified and warned. Not to mention the biological family that had completed all requirements and were all ready to get the kids home again. Well, my sweet, calm Zenna lost it when I got home and had to tell her. It was such a shock. She was ready to go home. This does not hurt my feelings, and many people don't understand this. She has so much with us it seems she would want to just stay here, but here's the thing, the children love their families no matter what. The family she missed was not just the siblings and mama; what I think she missed more were the relationships with the entire family—grandma, aunts, uncles, and cousins. No matter what, our family is important to us. Good or bad, they matter. She loves us and is happy, but family is family. Paul Pearsall is quoted as saying, "Our most basic instinct is not for survival but for family." I have seen the validity in these words as I love these children who have been neglected in all sorts of ways but still want to be with their families. This instinct is hard to explain or define. It just *is*.

Now we wait. I always dread this part, but I don't want the dread to distract me from all the blessings. This will most probably be our last foster child. I feel the end of this journey and am preparing for what God has in store for the next chapter. Usey and I were texting the other night and I told him that we were not going to foster anymore and that we felt like our time was done, and we would help another way. His response helped me so much. He said, "It is okay. You did so much good, I think it will be okay to take a break." I know I will always want to keep my hand in this arena, just from a different angle. I will be serving on the Foster Care Review Board in our county, and I hope to help bring more awareness to fostering. It isn't easy; it isn't all fun, but it is all worth it. When one child gets to know the Lord, it is worth it. When one family makes changes to benefit the children, it is worth it. When they get to see a better life and feel loved, it is worth it. The magnitude by which my own family has grown has been worth it. To see God's plans unfold and to recognize Him in it all is *totally* worth it! I realize I may never see many of these children again this side of heaven, but they each have left imprints on my heart that will last forever. I have been changed for the better. My family has been changed for the better. We will never be the same as we were before this journey. It has been dark, dirty, scary, lonely, confusing, sad, and overwhelmingly good. We can't be who we were before, nor would we want to be. He is refining us and molding us to His image and purpose. The process can be painful, but the final product is beautiful to behold.

Is God calling you to do something? Does it seem hard and overwhelming? Is Satan filling you with doubts and fears. Put your focus on the creator of the world, keep your eyes on Him, and just *go*! I pray you take that leap of faith and don't miss one single blessing He has planned for you and yours!

He is worth it!
You are worth it!

> *Lord, guard us and protect our hearts as we journey the path before us. May we keep our eyes on you and may you go before us in all things. May we walk in faith and not fear, using this time on earth for good and not for waste.*

Epilogue

After the completion of this book several things have happened to add some closure. After 7 years Devonta contacted us. He seems so good! It is evident that God has His hand on this child and that his plans are so much better than mine. He is in a place where he is growing and loved. He doesn't hoard anger in his heart and he will make it! His resiliency is noteworthy and admirable.

After living with us for a year and a half Zenna went home. She has been home for almost a year. She has been allowed to come for visits and remain in contact with us. She is making all A's and B's and is still the best thing ever!

God has reminded me over and over that His plans are so much better than mine. That even when things seem hopeless, He is my hope. When the battle seems lost, He has already won! It has been for the good!